CATS
BY JENNIE BREEDEN

ISBN 978-1480280502
Printed in USA
None of this is based
on any real people

DOGS HAVE OWNERS.
CATS HAVE CARETAKERS.

WHAT?

I'M DONE BEING CUDDLY NOW!

I'M F*CKING CUTE! PET ME!

NOW I HAVE HUMAN STINK ALL OVER ME.

YOU'VE CHANGED MY BRAND OF CAT FOOD. YOU HAVE NOW FORFEITED YOUR RIGHT TO BREATHE.

YOU EXPECT ME TO EAT THIS? ... SERIOUSLY?!
FLUFFY

YOU COULD FEED ME...OR NOT, I CAN ALWAYS EAT YOUR FACE.

I KNOW WHERE YOU KEEP YOUR UNDERWEAR.

I AM BEYOND INDIGNANT.

PET ME!
DON'T PET ME!
PET ME!
DON'T PET ME!

OH GOOD. I GOT YOUR ATTENTION. THAT IS ALL.

FLUSH IT AGAIN! FLUSH IT AGAIN!

WHACK!
WHACK!
WHACK!
AUTO MOUSE TOY
$99.99
BOX O' CAT TOYS

IT'S NOT MY FAULT YOU WALKED THROUGH A DOOR THAT I WAS SLEEPING IN.

IT'S EXHAUSTING BEING THIS CUTE.

CNIC
BOSTON BUTT
CLEAR PLATE
SPARE RIBS
LOIN
BACK FAT
BACON
SNORE

I DIDN'T DO IT! WHATEVER IT IS.

I MEANT TO DO THAT.

I LICK MY BUTT WITH THIS MOUTH.

YOU OPENED A CAN. IT **MUST** BE FOR **ME.**

MINE!

IT WAS MOVING.

I WILL EAT YOUR FACE.

THE SOONER YOU REALIZE I'M FABULOUS, THE EASIER YOUR LIFE WILL BE.

WHAT LITTER BOX?

I'M WASTING AWAY! I NEED A TREAT!

IT'S PAPER, IT MUST BE SAT UPON.

HOW CAN THAT BE MORE INTERESTING THAN ME?!

WHAT?

OH DARN...
THE SUNBEAM
GOT ME!

SCREW YOU.
I'M CUTE.

I'D PET YOU, BUT YOUR HAIR COMES OFF.

BUT CAT HAIR MAKES THAT OUTFIT BETTER.

IT WAS EATEN WHEN I FOUND IT.

YOU HAVE TWO HANDS! WHY AREN'T YOU USING THEM BOTH?

YOU ARE ALL BENEATH ME. NOW PET ME.

I AM UNAMUSED.

WHY AREN'T YOU PETTING ME?

YOU'RE JUST ENTERTAINING YOURSELF, YOU KNOW.

HMM, WHERE'S THE MOST TENDER SPOT FOR ME TO WALK ACROSS.

OH CRAP! HE WANTS TO PLAY AGAIN.

WHAT?!

TODAY IS THE DAY THAT I SHALL VANQUISH THE RED DOT OF DOOM!

SHE'S VACUUMING AGAIN.

I LOVE IT WHEN THEY DO LAUNDRY.

I'VE HIDDEN A HAIRBALL SOMEWHERE IN THIS HOUSE.

SHIT! SHE FOUND THE NAPALM!

WHAT DO YOU MEAN IT'S NOT A CHEW TOY?

WORSHIP ME.

SLEEP NOW!

BITCH! DON'T YOU KNOW I WILL CUT YOU?!?

EVERYTHING'S BETTER AFTER A GOOD NAP.

OH, WERE YOU ASLEEP?

I'M DELICIOUS!

WHO?
ME?!?

GODZILLA!

HOW COULD YOU THINK THAT I'D BE **OKAY** WITH THAT?!?

SELF CLEANING!
SELF CLEANING!

IF SHE ASKS ABOUT THE ARTICHOKE, TELL HER THAT I WAS IN GUAM.
MNW WHAT?

THERE'S A BUG IN THIS ROOM.
TWITCH! TWITCH!

YOU MEAN YOU DIDN'T PUT THIS OUT FOR ME TO SIT ON?
BILLS

NO AMOUNT OF TREATS WILL STOP ME FROM PEEING IN YOUR BED.

LOVE THE BUTT!
NGH!

AWESOME! I'VE GOT AN AUDIENCE. TIME FOR SOME BALL LICKIN'!

I CAN TASTE YOUR SOUL.

WARP SPEED
MR. SULU!

I'M TOO CUTE TO BE GUILTY!!

JUST BECAUSE I GOT MYSELF UP HERE, DOESN'T MEAN I KNOW HOW TO GET DOWN.

LOVE ME!!

HOW IS THAT FOOD?

I AM FLUFFY!
MASTER OF
ALL I SURVEY!

WHAT?

HOW CAN YOU NOT ADORE ME?!

THEY LOOK **BETTER** THAT WAY!

YOU'RE
KIDDING,
RIGHT?!

PET ME AND YOU MAY LIVE.

I'M COMFORTABLE. HOW CAN YOU NOT BE?

I KNOW YOU GUYS ARE HAVING FUN IN THERE WITHOUT ME!!

MORNING!

I WILL DINE ON YOUR ENTRAILS.

YOU KNOW I JUST LET YOU PRETEND TO RUN THINGS, RIGHT?

ARE YOU SURE THIS IS ALL I GET?
MUFFIN

WHY AREN'T YOU PETTING ME!?!

WHY LOOK, YOU GOT A LITTLE BED FOR YOURSELF. GOOD FOR YOU.
CAT BED
FLUFFY

NOT OKAY!!

I WILL IGNORE YOU, THEREFOR YOU WILL GIVE ME PETTIN'S.

HE BEATS US WITH STICKS. GOT ANY COOKIES?

A LITTLE MORE...

YOU LET THE LADY DO BAD THINGS TO ME!!

WHY IS SHE DIGGING THAT UP? I JUST BURIED IT!

IS SHE NICE?

SO, WHERE ARE YOU GONNA SIT?
ART IN PLACE

MOM, HELP! IT'S GOT ME!

KITTYKITTYKITTY!!
SHAKE!
SHAKE!
SHAKE
SHAKESHAKE!
SHAKE!

CRINKLY PAPER OF DOOM.
BITCH IS CRAZY!

I'M IN YOUR BED, STEALIN' YOUR WIFE.

TheDevilsPanties.com

27976346R00059

Made in the USA
Charleston, SC
28 March 2014